To the student

.... (enter your name here)

Welcome to this special Bible reading plan. I look forward to walking through God's Word with you in the coming weeks.

Each day you will read a brief passage of Scripture and either write out a verse or answer a question. Gradually you will read through whole books of the Bible.

I wanted to give you a few quick tips to help you get started and get the most out of the plan.

First, pray for God's blessing on your Bible reading, that He will open your eyes to understand His Word, and especially that He will show you more and more of the Lord Jesus Christ.

Second, write out some prayer points each week to remind you each day what to pray for. It might be to pray for your pastor, or your brother or sister, or a grandparent's illness, or something like that.

Third, why not try to memorize one of the verses each week? That way, you will build up a store of Bible verses in your heart and mind.

Last, talk to Mom and Dad about what you are reading. Show them what you are reading and writing and ask them any questions, or get them to test you on what you have read.

God bless and keep,

Pastor David Murray.

To Mom and Dad,

Like every Christian parent, I wanted my children to read the Bible. However, although I found numerous Bible reading plans for adults, I couldn't find what I wanted for my kids.

Some plans were way too ambitious and time-consuming; others just had random verses from here, there, and everywhere. Some had too much interactivity; others had too little. Some had one verse of Bible and one page of commentary!

I wanted my children to have a Bible reading plan that would be simple, systematic, interactive, do-able, and full of Bible. So...I wrote one myself. And when I shared the handouts on social media, I was taken aback by the interest and appreciation. Many asked for a book version, and you are holding the result.

Each book has about 100 days of Bible reading, each day has a brief question, and each week has an area for prayer points.

It shouldn't require more than five minutes a day, but, over a few years, your children will read and interact with much of the Bible. And they will end up not only with a memorable collection of Bible workbooks, but also a blessed habit of daily, systematic, interactive, and prayerful Bible reading.

I hope you will also talk to your children about the books. Why not have a weekly discussion about the readings and answers, and use the opportunity to not only keep them accountable but to develop another holy habit, that of freely discussing the Word of God with one another.

Sometimes we'll skip some passages that are especially difficult for children. They can be read and studied when the children are older and better able to profit from them.

May God bless these plans so that it may be said of all our children: "From childhood you have known the Holy Scriptures, which are able to make you wise for salvation through faith which is in Christ Jesus" (2 Tim. 3:15).

Pastor David Murray.

Week 1: Genesis 21

PRAYER POINTS

--   --

--   --

--   --

--   --

SUNDAY
Reading: Genesis 21:1-5
Question: How old was Abraham when Isaac was born? (v. 5)

MONDAY
Reading: Genesis 21:6-8
Write Out: Genesis 21:6

TUESDAY
Reading: Genesis 21:9-11
Question: What did Sarah want Abraham to do with Hagar and Ishmael? (v. 10)

WEDNESDAY
Reading: Genesis 21:12-16
Write Out: Genesis 21:15

THURSDAY
Reading: Genesis 21:17-21
Question: What did the angel of God say to Hagar? (v. 17-18)

FRIDAY
Reading: Genesis 21:22-26
Question: What were the men fighting over? (v. 25)

SATURDAY
Reading: Genesis 21:27-31
Write Out: Genesis 21:31

----

*Extra Question: What did the Egyptians notice about Abraham?
(Genesis 21:22). Do people think this about you?*

Week 2: Genesis 21-23

PRAYER POINTS

--------------------------------------   --------------------------------------

--------------------------------------   --------------------------------------

--------------------------------------   --------------------------------------

--------------------------------------   --------------------------------------

SUNDAY
Reading: Genesis 21:32-34
Question: What did Abraham do at Beersheba? (v. 33)

MONDAY
Reading: Genesis 22:1-4
Question: What did God command Abraham to do with Isaac? (v. 2)

TUESDAY
Reading: Genesis 22:5-8
Write Out: Genesis 22:8

WEDNESDAY
Reading: Genesis 22:9-11
Write Out: Genesis 22:11

THURSDAY
Reading: Genesis 22:12-14
Question: What did Abraham call the place? (v. 14)

FRIDAY
Reading: Genesis 22:15-19
Write Out: Genesis 22:18

SATURDAY
Reading: Genesis 23:1-6
Write Out: Genesis 23:1

Extra Question: Genesis 22:18 is a prophecy. What does it predict? (See Galatians 3:8).

Week 3: Genesis 23-24

PRAYER POINTS

-------------------------------------   -------------------------------------

-------------------------------------   -------------------------------------

-------------------------------------   -------------------------------------

-------------------------------------   -------------------------------------

SUNDAY
Reading: Genesis 23:7-11
Question: What did Abraham ask for? (v. 9)

MONDAY
Reading: Genesis 23:12-16
Question: How much did Abraham pay for the land? (v. 16)

TUESDAY
Reading: Genesis 23:17-20
Write Out: Genesis 23:20

WEDNESDAY
Reading: Genesis 24:1-4
Write Out: Genesis 24:1

THURSDAY
Reading: Genesis 24:5-9
Question: What did God promise Abraham? (v. 7)

FRIDAY
Reading: Genesis 24:10-14
Write Out: Genesis 24:12

SATURDAY
Reading: Genesis 24:15-20
Question: What did the servant ask for? (v. 17)

Extra Question: Who did Abraham want Isaac to marry? (Genesis 24:3-4)

Week 4: Genesis 24-25

PRAYER POINTS

--   --

--   --

--   --

--   --

SUNDAY
Reading: Genesis 24:21-26
Write Out: Genesis 24:26

MONDAY
Reading: Genesis 24:27-31
Write Out: Genesis 24:27

TUESDAY
Reading: Genesis 24:32-35
Question: What was the reason for Abraham's wealth? (v. 35)

WEDNESDAY
Reading: Genesis 24:36-41
Write Out: Genesis 24:37

THURSDAY
Reading: Genesis 24:42-44
Question: How was the servant to know who was to be Isaac's future wife? (v. 43-44)

FRIDAY
Reading: Genesis 24:45-48
Write Out: Genesis 24:48

SATURDAY
Reading: Genesis 24:49-53
Write Out: Genesis 24:50

Extra Question: Who led Abraham's servant to the right wife for his son? (Genesis 24:48)

Week 5: Genesis 24-25

PRAYER POINTS

--   --

--   --

--   --

--   --

SUNDAY
Reading: Genesis 24:54-59
Question: What did they ask Rebekah? (v. 58)

MONDAY
Reading: Genesis 24:60-67
Write Out: Genesis 24:60

TUESDAY
Reading: Genesis 25:1-6
Question: What did Abraham give to Isaac? (v. 5)

WEDNESDAY
Reading: Genesis 25:7-11
Write Out: Genesis 25:11

THURSDAY
Reading: Genesis 25:12-18
Question: How old was Ishmael when he died? (v. 17)

FRIDAY
Reading: Genesis 25:19-23
Write Out: Genesis 25:22

SATURDAY
Reading: Genesis 25:24-28
Write Out: Genesis 25:28

Extra Question: What should we do when we face struggles?
(Genesis 25:22)

Week 6: Genesis 25-26

PRAYER POINTS

---   ---

---   ---

---   ---

---   ---

SUNDAY
Reading: Genesis 25:29-34
Question: What did Esau do to his birthright? (v. 33)

MONDAY
Reading: Genesis 26:1-5
Write Out: Genesis 26:4

TUESDAY
Reading: Genesis 26:6-10
Question: How did Isaac describe his wife? (v. 7)

WEDNESDAY
Reading: Genesis 26:11-16
Write Out: Genesis 26:12

THURSDAY
Reading: Genesis 26:17-20
Question: What were the men fighting over? (v. 20)

FRIDAY
Reading: Genesis 26:21-25
Write Out: Genesis 26:24

SATURDAY
Reading: Genesis 26:26-30
Question: What did people see about Isaac? (v. 28)

Extra Question: What do you think it meant that Isaac called upon the name of the Lord? (Genesis 26:25)

Week 7: Genesis 26-27

PRAYER POINTS

---   ---

---   ---

---   ---

---   ---

SUNDAY
Reading: Genesis 26:31-35
Question: What caused Isaac and Rebekah such grief? (v. 34-35)

MONDAY
Reading: Genesis 27:1-5
Write Out: Genesis 27:4

TUESDAY
Reading: Genesis 27:6-10
Write Out: Genesis 27:10

WEDNESDAY
Reading: Genesis 27:11-14
Question: What did Rebekah say about the curse on lying?
(v. 13)

THURSDAY
Reading: Genesis 27:15-19
Write Out: Genesis 27:18

FRIDAY
Reading: Genesis 27:20-25
Question: How did Jacob explain the speed of the meal? (v. 20)

SATURDAY
Reading: Genesis 27:26-29
Write Out: Genesis 27:29

----

*Extra Question: Who is to blame for the family strife in Genesis
27?*

Week 8: Genesis 27-28

PRAYER POINTS

--   --

--   --

--   --

--   --

SUNDAY
Reading: Genesis 27:30-33
Question: How did Isaac react when he heard Esau's voice? (v. 33)

MONDAY
Reading: Genesis 27:34-37
Write Out: Genesis 27:35

TUESDAY
Reading: Genesis 27:38-40
Question: What did Esau ask for? (v. 38)

WEDNESDAY
Reading: Genesis 27:41-46
Write Out: Genesis 27:43

THURSDAY
Reading: Genesis 28:1-5
Write Out: Genesis 28:4

FRIDAY
Reading: Genesis 28:6-9
Write Out: What did Esau do to annoy his parents? (v. 8-9)

SATURDAY
Reading: Genesis 28:10-12
Write Out: Genesis 28:12

Extra Question: Why was it so important that Israelites not marry non Israelites? (See 2 Corinthians 6:14)

Week 9: Genesis 28-29

PRAYER POINTS

------------------------------------   ------------------------------------

------------------------------------   ------------------------------------

------------------------------------   ------------------------------------

------------------------------------   ------------------------------------

SUNDAY
Reading: Genesis 28:13-15
Question: Who stood at the top of the ladder? (v. 13)

MONDAY
Reading: Genesis 28:16-22
Write Out: Genesis 28:16

TUESDAY
Reading: Genesis 29:1-3
Question: What was on the well? (v. 3)

WEDNESDAY
Reading: Genesis 29:4-8
Write Out: Genesis 29:6

THURSDAY
Reading: Genesis 29:9-14
Write Out: Genesis 29:11

FRIDAY
Reading: Genesis 29:15-20
Question: Why did the time seem so short to Jacob? (v. 20)

SATURDAY
Reading: Genesis 29:21-25
Question: How did Laban trick Jacob? (v. 23-25)

Extra Question: How does loving God change our relationship with Him? (Think about Genesis 29:20)

Week 10: Genesis 29-30

PRAYER POINTS

--------------------------------------   --------------------------------------

--------------------------------------   --------------------------------------

--------------------------------------   --------------------------------------

--------------------------------------   --------------------------------------

SUNDAY
Reading: Genesis 29:26-30
Question: Who did Jacob love most? (v. 30)

MONDAY
Reading: Genesis 29:31-35
Write Out: Genesis 29:35

TUESDAY
Reading: Genesis 30:1-6
Write Out: Genesis 30:1

WEDNESDAY
Reading: Genesis 30:7-13
Write Out: Genesis 30:13

THURSDAY
Reading: Genesis 30:14-17
Question: What did Leah buy Jacob's love with? (v. 16)

FRIDAY
Reading: Genesis 30:18-21
Write Out: Genesis 30:19

SATURDAY
Reading: Genesis 30:22-26
Write Out: Genesis 30:22

Extra Question: Do you think Jacob had a happy family? Why or why not?

Week 11: Genesis 30-31

PRAYER POINTS

------------------------------------   ------------------------------------

------------------------------------   ------------------------------------

------------------------------------   ------------------------------------

------------------------------------   ------------------------------------

SUNDAY
Reading: Genesis 30:27-30
Question: What had Laban learned? (v. 27)

MONDAY
Reading: Genesis 30:31-34
Write Out: Genesis 30:34

TUESDAY
Reading: Genesis 30:35-39
Question: Describe the colors of the flocks. (v. 39)

WEDNESDAY
Reading: Genesis 30:40-43
Write Out: Genesis 30:43

THURSDAY
Reading: Genesis 31:1-3
Write Out: Genesis 31:3

FRIDAY
Reading: Genesis 31:4-9
Question: Describe Jacob's working. (v. 6)

SATURDAY
Reading: Genesis 31:10-12
Question: Who spoke to Jacob and how? (v. 11)

Extra Question: Who decided if Jacob or Laban should prosper? (Genesis 31:9)

Week 12: Genesis 31

PRAYER POINTS

---   ---

---   ---

---   ---

---   ---

SUNDAY
Reading: Genesis 31:13-16
Write Out: Genesis 31:13

MONDAY
Reading: Genesis 31:17-20
Question: How did Jacob leave Laban? (v. 20)

TUESDAY
Reading: Genesis 31:21-24
Write Out: Genesis 31:24

WEDNESDAY
Reading: Genesis 31:25-30
Question: What did God say to Laban? (v. 29)

THURSDAY
Reading: Genesis 31:31-35
Question: Where were Laban's idols? (v. 32, 34)

FRIDAY
Reading: Genesis 31:36-39
Write Out: Genesis 31:36

SATURDAY
Reading: Genesis 31:40-42
Question: How did Jacob describe God? (v. 42)

Extra Question: What do the idols tell you about Rachel's spiritual condition at the time?

Week 13: Genesis 31-32

PRAYER POINTS

---------------------------------------   ---------------------------------------

---------------------------------------   ---------------------------------------

---------------------------------------   ---------------------------------------

---------------------------------------   ---------------------------------------

SUNDAY
Reading: Genesis 31:43-46
Write Out: Genesis 31:44

MONDAY
Reading: Genesis 31:47-50
Question: Who was the witness to the covenant? (v. 50)

TUESDAY
Reading: Genesis 31:51-55
Write Out: Genesis 31:53

WEDNESDAY

Reading: Genesis 32:1-5

Question: Who met Jacob? (v. 1)

THURSDAY

Reading: Genesis 32:6-8

Question: What did Jacob do when he heard Esau was coming?
(v. 7)

FRIDAY

Reading: Genesis 32:9-12

Write Out: Genesis 32:10a (just the first part of the verse)

SATURDAY

Reading: Genesis 32:13-16

Write Out: Genesis 32:13

----

*Extra Question: What did Jacob mean when he said he was not
worthy of the least of God's mercies? (Genesis 32:10)*

Week 14: Genesis 32-33

PRAYER POINTS

-- --

-- --

-- --

-- --

SUNDAY
Reading: Genesis 32:17-20
Question: What did Jacob hope the presents would do to Esau?
(v. 20)

MONDAY
Reading: Genesis 32:21-24
Write Out: Genesis 32:24

TUESDAY
Reading: Genesis 32:25-28
Question: Why did the Angel rename Jacob? (v. 28)

WEDNESDAY
Reading: Genesis 32:29-32
Write Out: Genesis 32:30

THURSDAY
Reading: Genesis 33:1-4
Question: What did Esau do when he met Jacob? (v. 4)

FRIDAY
Reading: Genesis 33:5-9
Write Out: Genesis 33:9

SATURDAY
Reading: Genesis 33:10-11
Write Out: Genesis 33:11

Extra Question: Who did Jacob wrestle with? (Genesis 32:30)

Note to parents: You'll notice that next week we skip Chapter 34. This is due to the sensitive nature of the content. Feel free to go over it with your children if you believe they are ready and would benefit from its study.

Week 15: Genesis 33-35

PRAYER POINTS

------------------------------------   ------------------------------------

------------------------------------   ------------------------------------

------------------------------------   ------------------------------------

------------------------------------   ------------------------------------

SUNDAY
Reading: Genesis 33:12-15
Question: Where do we find grace? (v. 15)

MONDAY
Reading: Genesis 33:16-20
Write out: Genesis 33:20

TUESDAY
Reading: Genesis 35:1-5
Write Out: Genesis 35:3

WEDNESDAY
Reading: Genesis 35:6-8
Question: What did Jacob call the place he built the altar? (v. 7)

THURSDAY
Reading: Genesis 35:9-12
Write Out: Genesis 35:11

FRIDAY
Reading: Genesis 35:13-15
Question: What did Jacob call the name of the place God spoke with him? (v. 15)

SATURDAY
Reading: Genesis 35:16-20
Question: What did Jacob call Rachel's last son? (v. 18)

Extra Question: What does the name Ben-Oni mean? What does the name Benjamin mean? (Genesis 35:18. Hint: These answers are probably in the footnotes of your Bible).

Week 16: Genesis 35-36

PRAYER POINTS

---------------------------------------   ---------------------------------------

---------------------------------------   ---------------------------------------

---------------------------------------   ---------------------------------------

SUNDAY
Reading: Genesis 35:21-22, 27-29
Question: How old was Isaac when he died? (v. 28)

MONDAY
Reading: Genesis 36:1-5
Question: Where did Esau take his wives from? (v. 2)

TUESDAY
Reading: Genesis 36:6-8
Question: Where did Esau live? (v. 8)

Extra Question: What do you think was wrong with Esau marrying Canaanite wives? (Genesis 36:1)

KidsBibleReading.com

More in this series:

Volume 1: Genesis 1-20

Volume 2: Genesis 21-36

Volume 3: Genesis 37-50

Volume 4: Matthew 1-14

Volume 5: Matthew 15-28

Depending on the response to these Bible reading plans, more volumes will be released every six months. Please recommend to others or leave an Amazon review.

Buy more on Amazon.com or visit KidsBibleReading.com for wholesale pricing for your school or church.